D1165085

Cesar Chavez

Jennifer Strand

abdopublishing.com

Published by Abdo Zoom™, PO Box 398166, Minneapolis, Minnesota 55439. Copyright © 2017 by Abdo Consulting Group, Inc. International copyrights reserved in all countries. No part of this book may be reproduced in any form without written permission from the publisher. Abdo Zoom™ is a trademark and logo of Abdo Consulting Group, Inc.

Printed in the United States of America, North Mankato, Minnesota
072016
092016

THIS BOOK CONTAINS RECYCLED MATERIALS

Cover Photo: Alan Greth/AP Images
Interior Photos: Alan Greth/AP Images, 1; Arthur Schatz/The LIFE Picture Collection/Getty Images, 4, 8; Bob Parent/Hulton Archive/Getty Images, 5; Dorothea Lange/Library of Congress, 6–7; AP Images, 9, 13; Reed Saxon/AP Images, 10–11; George Widman/AP Images, 11; Bettmann/Getty Images, 14; Cathy Murphy/Getty Images, 16–17; Charles Knoblock/AP Images, 17; Jim Bourdier/AP Images, 19

Editor: Brienna Rossiter
Series Designer: Madeline Berger
Art Direction: Dorothy Toth

Publisher's Cataloging-in-Publication Data
Names: Strand, Jennifer, author.
Title: Cesar Chavez / by Jennifer Strand.
Description: Minneapolis, MN : Abdo Zoom, [2017] | Series: Legendary leaders | Includes bibliographical references and index.
Identifiers: LCCN 2016941391 | ISBN 9781680792362 (lib. bdg.) | ISBN 9781680794045 (ebook) | 9781680794939 (Read-to-me ebook)
Subjects: LCSH: Chavez, Cesar, 1927-1993--Juvenile literature. | Labor leaders--United States--Biography--Juvenile literature. | Mexican Americans-Biography--Juvenile literature. | Mexican American agricultural laborers--History--Juvenile literature. | Agricultural laborers--Labor unions--United States--History--Juvenile literature. | United Farm Workers--History--Juvenile literature.
Classification: DDC 331.88/13092 [B]--dc23
LC record available at http://lccn.loc.gov/2016941391

Table of Contents

Cesar Chavez was a **union** leader.

He helped workers be treated fairly.
He led peaceful protests.

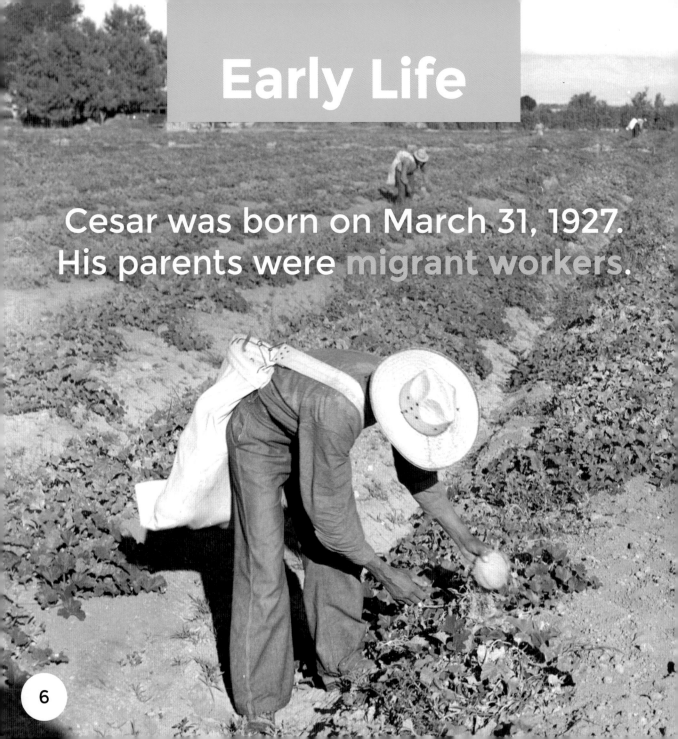

Early Life

Cesar was born on March 31, 1927. His parents were migrant workers.

They planted and picked crops.
It was hard work.
But they were not paid much.

Chavez planned a **strike** for grape pickers.

They asked to be paid more. But they stayed peaceful.

Chavez also started a boycott.

He asked people
to stop buying grapes.

History Maker

In 1966 Chavez led a march.
Many workers walked across
California. They asked people
to support the strike.

The march lasted 25 days. It worked. Grape growers agreed to pay the workers more.

Chavez led more
strikes and boycotts.
In 1975 a law was passed.

It made conditions
better for workers.

Chavez helped people work together to be treated fairly.
He died on April 23, 1993.
But his union still helps workers.

Cesar Chavez

Born: March 31, 1927

Birthplace: Yuma, Arizona

Known For: Chavez was a union leader. He helped migrant workers be treated fairly.

Died: April 23, 1993

Key Dates

1927: Cesario Estrada Chavez is born on March 31.

1962: Chavez forms the National Farm Workers Association (NFWA) with Dolores Huerta.

1965: The NFWA begins its first grape boycott.

1966: Chavez begins his march to Sacramento, California.

1988: Chavez holds his "Fast for Life."

1993: Chavez dies on April 23.

Glossary

boycott - to refuse to buy or use something until changes are made.

migrant worker - a person who goes from place to place to do jobs.

protest - an event where people show they oppose something.

strike - when workers refuse to do their jobs until changes are made.

union - a group of people who work together to protect each other's rights.

Booklinks

For more information
on **Cesar Chavez**, please visit
booklinks.abdopublishing.com

Z∞m In on Biographies!

Learn even more with the Abdo Zoom
Biographies database. Check out
abdozoom.com for more information.

Index